The Stuff Dreams Are Made Of.

Proudly supplying the equipment that helps the dreams of future champions come true. Since 1884.

Louisville Slugger®

Louisville Slugger®

NEW YORK METS

BILL SHANNON

BONANZA BOOKS

New York

First published in 1991 by Bonanza Books, distributed by Outlet Book
Company, Inc., a Random House Company, 225 Park Avenue South,
New York, New York 10003, by arrangement with MBKA.

ACKNOWLEDGMENTS

Majority of Player Photographs by Tom Dipace
Additional thanks to:
John Broggi—JKJ Sports Collectibles, Inc.
National Baseball Hall of Fame & Museum, Inc.

Printed and bound in the United States of America

Library of Congress Cataloging-in-Publication Data

Shannon, Bill.
    The New York Mets / by Bill Shannon.
       p.   cm. — (Louisville Slugger)
    Summary: An overview of the New York Mets baseball team,
discussing its history, last season, great moments, records, and
prospects.
    ISBN 0-517-05792-1
    1. New York Mets (Baseball team)—Juvenile literature.
[1. New York Mets (Baseball team)] I. Title. II. Series.
GV875.N45S48 1991
796.357′64′097471—dc20   90-28327
                                                CIP
                                                 AC

ISBN 0-517-05792-1

8 7 6 5 4 3 2 1

CONTENTS

BUD HARRELSON
MANAGER

Davey Johnson, one of the winningest managers in major league history and the first manager ever to manage 1,000 games for the Mets, was dismissed on May 29 in Cincinnati. Bud Harrelson took over a club that was 20-22. Under Harrelson the Mets played at a .592 pace the rest of the season, rose briefly into first place a couple of times, and made a race of the NL East—but still finished four games off the pace of the Pirates. Critical to the shape of the pennant race was a doubleheader in Pittsburgh on September 12: the Pirates won both games, 1-0 and 1-0. Harrelson, with a total major league managerial experience of 120 games, will now try to prepare his club from the start of spring training. Harrelson is a big part of Met history, having played shortstop for the fabled 1969 world champions and the 1973 National League pennant winners. He was signed as a free agent on June 7, 1963, and has been with the Mets virtually ever since, as a player, coach, broadcaster, and now manager. He played with the club from 1965 to 1977, appearing in 1,322 games as a shortstop. After brief stints with the Phillies and Rangers, he returned as a coach under George Bamberger, worked for a season as an announcer on the club's cable telecasts, and became a coach under Johnson in 1985. Then he became the 12th field manager in the history of the club. As a player, he was named to the National League All-Star team twice (in 1970 and 1971). Now he has the opportunity to manage the NL team in an All-Star game. All he has to do is to win the pennant.

DAVID CONE
PITCHER

Over the last two-thirds of the 1990 season, David Cone had his finest "season" to date. In a span of 22 games he was 13-6 and struck out 176 men in 164 innings. His closing burst enabled him to lead the National League in strikeouts with 233, and to nip Nolan Ryan for the major-league strikeout crown. He became the first Met pitcher since Doc Gooden (1985) to lead the NL in strikeouts. At one point Cone struck out 10 or more hitters in four straight starts (June 30 to July 19). He had a personal six-game winning streak, which was snapped by the Cardinals on July 28, when he lost 1-0. During his final 22 starts, Cone lowered his earned run average from a bloated 6.27 to a season-ending 3.23, a somewhat remarkable recovery. He also notched a new career high in strikeouts with 13 against the Giants in San Francisco on August 18, allowing only seven hits and one earned run. (He had struck out 12 in a game four previous times.) With the fast finish he became a 14-game winner for the second year in a row, and he closed out the season by winning his last two starts without allowing an earned run, scattering only five hits over 17 innings and striking out 19. Cone might have had an even better record if he hadn't been rained out of two starts during his hot streak. One of his personal highlights of 1990 occurred on August 1 against Montreal, when he became the first pitcher in Mets' history to collect a pinch hit, singling against the Expos' Dale Mohorcic. In 1991 the Mets hope that they see the Cone of the last two-thirds of last season, not the one who was 1-4 in his first nine starts.

Age: 28			Bats: Left					Throws: Right		
	W	L	SV	G	CG	IP	HA	BB	SO	ERA
1990	14	10	0	31	6	211.2	177	65	233	3.23
Career	53	27	1	132	22	784.2	654	276	725	3.14

RON DARLING
PITCHER

Ron Darling can only hope that 1991 is a better year for him than 1990 was. Unsettled by continuous trade rumors and relegated to the bullpen for much of the season, Darling had easily the worst year of his career. He began the season in the starting rotation but was 1-3 with a 6.84 ERA on May 15. He was then shipped to the bullpen. He made four straight relief appearances before he got another start. That came on June 13 in the second game of a doubleheader against the Cubs at Wrigley Field. He pitched six innings and won the game, a 9-6 victory. Darling made no secret of his unhappiness over his ill-defined role, but even the Mets' managerial change did little to relieve his distress, since Bud Harrelson continued the Davey Johnson pattern of shuffling him back and forth between the starting rotation and the bullpen. Overall, Darling appeared in 33 games, 15 of them in relief. As a reliever, he was 1-2 with a 3.99 ERA, with 10 walks and 23 strikeouts in 29⅓ innings. His one relief win came on April 15 against the Atlanta Braves in New York, when he worked one perfect inning. He continued to be the toughest right-hander in the league on base runners, picking off five, three of them at second base. What the 30-year-old is hoping for is that he will be returned to the starting rotation for the Mets in 1991, but at this writing the Mets still had one starter too many.

Age: 30			Bats: Right						Throws: Right	
	W	L	SV	G	CG	IP	HA	BB	SO	ERA
1990	7	9	0	33	1	126.0	135	44	99	4.50
Career	94	64	0	240	25	1517.2	1377	586	1090	3.48

SID FERNANDEZ

PITCHER

For the second time in three seasons, left-hander Sid Fernandez held National League hitters to the lowest batting average allowed by any pitcher in the National League. He turned the trick in 1988, when the league batted only .191 against him, as well as in 1990, when the league batted just .200, with 130 hits in 650 at-bats. In 1989 he finished second (.198), and over his career opposing hitters are batting only .204 against him. Nonetheless, Fernandez is one of the most frustrating pitchers on the Mets, since he is not a consistent winner despite the fact that batters don't seem to be able to hit him. In his final 10 starts last season, he won only once, lost six times, and had three no-decisions. Earlier he went through a five-game stretch (from April 28 to May 20) when he won only once, with three losses and a no-decision. He also missed two starts in late June with a muscle strain in his left elbow. On the plus side, Fernandez threw two complete games in 1990, including one on August 10 against the Cubs when he won, 5-1, without issuing a walk. It was only the third time in his career that he pitched a complete game without issuing a walk. Fernandez had four double-figure strikeout games during 1990 and finished fifth in the league with 181 strikeouts. In 1991, Fernandez, now 28, could be a key to whether or not the Mets remain one of the premiere teams in the NL East. If he can win with any regularity, the Mets could be the team to beat without the potent offense of previous seasons. But he must overcome the nasty habit of allowing just enough runs *not* to win.

Age: 28			Bats: Left						Throws: Left	
	W	L	SV	G	CG	IP	HA	BB	SO	ERA
1990	9	14	0	30	2	179.1	130	67	181	3.46
Career	78	59	1	199	17	1212.1	894	491	1153	3.26

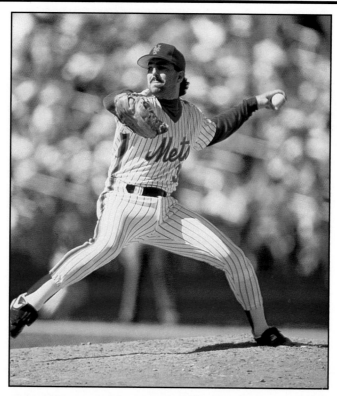

JOHN FRANCO
RELIEF PITCHER

By most standards, left-handed reliever John Franco had a very successful season, leading the league in saves with 33. But the man for whom he was traded, Randy Myers, wound up on the world championship team (although he didn't gain many individual honors). Franco was workmanlike rather than spectacular in 1990. He gained his 33 saves in 39 opportunities, posting the second highest total of his career and setting a Mets' club record in the process. The previous best was 31 by Jesse Orosco in 1984. He won his second Relief Man of the Year title, having also won it in 1988, when he led the NL with a career-high 39 saves for the Reds. He started the season with six saves in his first seven appearances and allowed just one run in the month of April. In July, Franco had a streak in which he saved all nine games in which he appeared, yielding only seven hits in 11⅓ innings. From July 4 through September 1 he had 17 straight saves. He didn't lose a game until September 5, when he was beaten by the Pirates, 1-0, in the opening game of a doubleheader at Three Rivers Stadium. The Mets will probably need that kind of performance from him again in 1991 to remain a prime contender in the division. The Mets must also improve their set-up relief staff, since late in the year Franco was frequently required to pitch two (or more) innings to protect a game.

Age: 30				Bats: Left				Throws: Left	
	W	L	SV	G	CG	IP	HA	BB	SO	ERA
1990	5	3	33	55	0	67.2	66	21	56	2.53
Career	47	33	181	448	0	595.2	526	231	423	2.49

DWIGHT GOODEN

PITCHER

Doc Gooden, the third youngest pitcher in the modern era to win 100 games (and the 100-game winner with the second-best percentage at the time he won his 100th game), was a question mark when the 1990 season began. That was because of the shoulder injury, diagnosed as a muscle tear in the back of his right shoulder, that had curtailed his 1989 season. But after a bit of a slow start, Gooden was the best pitcher on the Mets through most of the season and was picked as the toughest pitcher in the league by opposing batters. He began with a 3-5 start and had a 4.37 ERA on June 2. But from that point on, Gooden was almost impossible to beat and appeared to have regained much of his old form. In a game against the Pirates in Pittsburgh, he was recorded as throwing at 100 miles-per-hour. After June 2 he lost only twice during the entire remainder of the season: on August 4 to St. Louis and on October 3 to Pittsburgh. From June 12 through July 17 he posted seven straight wins in seven starts, matching a career high. After a no-decision, he then won his eighth straight before losing to the Cardinals. Then came another eight-game winning streak before the final defeat by the Pirates. He tied for second in the NL in strikeouts (223) and was one of four Met pitchers in the top ten in strikeouts. As a hitter, Gooden had a four-RBI game against the Dodgers on May 11. In that game he also struck out 15 Dodgers, the second highest total of his career (and he pitched only seven innings). With Gooden back as a premiere pitcher, the Mets figure to remain at or near the top of the division, if the remainder of the staff can maintain its level of performance. However, Gooden did win some games last season in which he allowed a lot of runs, and he may not have that luxury in 1991.

Age: 26			Bats: Right						Throws: Right	
	W	L	SV	G	CG	IP	HA	BB	SO	ERA
1990	19	7	0	34	2	232.2	229	70	223	3.83
Career	119	46	1	211	54	1523.2	1282	449	1391	2.82

JEFF MUSSELMAN

PITCHER

Jeff Musselman, who started the 1989 season with the Toronto Blue Jays, rapidly became an integral part of the Mets' bullpen after being acquired on July 31 of that year. He appeared in 20 games for New York and finished with a 3-2 record. He started last season in New York but was optioned to Tidewater in mid-July, being recalled to the Mets on September 4. A left-hander, Musselman is called upon primarily to get a couple of key outs in given situations. He started 1990 strongly, allowing only one run in his first five outings (a total of five innings) and did not allow a run over a four-game stretch from May 16 to May 27. He was outstanding at preventing inherited runners from scoring. During the season he appeared in games with a total of 16 runners aboard, and only one scored. That, oddly, was the last one he inherited; the previous 15 runners, including two runners on base seven times, did not score. At Tidewater, the Mets' triple-A affiliate, Musselman was used exclusively as a starter. In 10 starts, he had a 4-3 record and posted a seven-inning complete-game shutout. In 56⅓ innings, he allowed 60 hits and 22 earned runs and struck out 31 while walking 16. However, he cannot expect a spot in the starting rotation with the Mets. Rather, he is likely to continue as a left-handed specialist and as a potential set-up man for John Franco. The additional innings he pitched last year at triple-A helped to sharpen him for work this season with the Mets.

Age: 27				Bats: Left					Throws: Left	
	W	L	SV	G	CG	IP	HA	BB	SO	ERA
1990	3	2	0	28	0	32.0	40	11	14	5.63
Career	23	15	3	142	0	248.2	249	123	125	4.31

HUBIE BROOKS

RIGHT FIELD

Brooks made his major league debut as a third baseman with the New York Mets in 1980. The club moved him to shortstop in mid-1984, and he responded with 16 home runs and 73 RBIs, as the Mets became surprise contenders. Immediately following the season, he was traded to the Expos as part of the package that brought Gary Carter to New York. Brooks flourished in Montreal. In 1985 he became the first National League shortstop since Ernie Banks to drive in 100 runs. In 1986 injuries cut him down in mid-season while he was hitting .340. Brooks was a consistent run producer throughout his Expo career, but his tenure with them ended badly. He was unhappy with the way he was utilized by Montreal skipper Buck Rodgers throughout 1989. In a move he did not approve of, he was switched to right field. During the September stretch drive, Rodgers platooned Brooks with rookie Larry Walker as the Expos fell from the pennant race. That was especially galling for Brooks, who had been the club's top clutch hitter. He refused to entertain a Montreal contract offer and the Dodgers signed him as a free agent during the winter of 1989. They had been after his productive bat for years. Brooks met L.A.'s expectations by matching his career high in home runs (20) and posting his second-highest RBI total (91). After the Dodgers signed both Darryl Strawberry and Bret Butler as free agents, Brooks became expendable. He was traded to the Mets for lefthanded pitcher Bob Ojeda on December 15.

Age: 34				Bats: Right					Throws: Right			
	G	AB	H	2B	3B	HR	R	RBI	BB	SO	SB	AVG.
1990	153	568	151	28	1	20	74	91	33	108	2	.266
Career	1351	5082	1395	252	30	123	561	700	318	860	57	.274

ALEJANDRO PENA
RELIEF PITCHER

Acquired in the off-season trade that also brought first baseman Mike Marshall from the Dodgers for Juan Samuel, Alejandro Pena made the deal look a lot better from the Mets' point of view with a strong finish in 1990. In mid-August, Pena had a bloated 4.44 ERA—and that was down from a high of 4.99 in late June. But over his final 17 appearances, he allowed just one run. During that period, he cut his ERA down to 3.20, to finish the season with some respectable numbers. Perhaps his best game in that stretch came on September 25, when he pitched four shutout innings against the Expos in Montreal and was the winning pitcher in a 3-1 Mets' victory. Overall, he did fairly well despite his rocky start. Pena had five saves in five opportunities, with his fifth coming on October 3, the season's final day, when he protected Frank Viola's 20th victory, a 6-3 triumph over the Pirates at Pittsburgh. His first save as a Met came on April 16 in Chicago, when he worked three innings behind Viola. He worked another three-inning stint on May 22 at Los Angeles, when he saved an 8-3 win for Bob Ojeda. His next two saves came at home, on July 30 against Atlanta and on August 12 against Chicago. Pena is an experienced bullpen hand who now has a 41-41 career record and 37 career saves. Odds are he will see a good deal more service this season than he did last year with the Mets, serving as a right-handed alternate for Franco. Over his final 28 games last season, he allowed only 10 earned runs in 45⅓ innings, for an ERA of 1.99. That kind of work tends to get you more work.

Age: 31				Bats: Right				Throws: Right		
	W	L	SV	G	CG	IP	HA	BB	SO	ERA
1990	3	3	5	52	0	76.0	71	22	76	3.20
Career	41	41	37	333	12	845.0	764	266	647	2.95

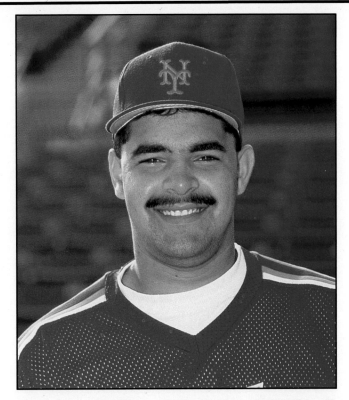

JULIO VALERA

PITCHER

While it remains to be seen whether he is ready for a steady diet of major league work, right-hander Julio Valera may be the next top Met pitcher. Now 22, Valera has shown a high strikeout ratio in the minor leagues, but he obviously suffered from nerves during his brief three-game trial late last season with New York. In those three games he worked 13 innings and recorded only four strikeouts. But during the triple-A season at Tidewater he fanned 133 in 158 innings. In 1989 at Jackson (double-A) Valera had 107 strikeouts in 137⅓ innings, and in 1988 at the A level he struck out 144 in 191⅓ innings. Indications are that he will get some Ks in the majors. He was recalled from Tidewater on August 30 and made his major league debut two days later, getting the win in a 6-5 victory over the Giants. He worked six innings, allowing five hits, three earned runs, and two walks and striking out three. His second start was a complete disaster. On September 6 at Pittsburgh, he worked only two innings and allowed eight hits and five runs (four of them earned), walked two, and struck out one. His final start was a no-decision against St. Louis, although the Mets won the game. He worked five innings, allowing three runs and seven hits. In his 24 starts at Tidewater, Valera had nine complete games, two of them shutouts. He also had a 14-strikeout game against Scranton–Wilkes-Barre, and in his last start before his recall to the Mets he threw a two-hitter against Indianapolis. He has an excellent chance of making the club in spring training and of working his way in as a middle-relief man.

Age: 22				Bats: Right				Throws: Right	
	W	L	SV	G	CG	IP	HA	BB	SO	ERA
1990	1	1	0	3	0	13.0	20	7	4	6.92
Career	1	1	0	3	0	13.0	20	7	4	6.92

FRANK VIOLA
PITCHER

Celebrating his first full season in his hometown, Frank Viola became only the 18th pitcher in major league history to win 20 or more games in a season in both leagues. Viola was 24-7 in his Cy Young season with Minnesota in 1988. His 20 victories in 1990 were the most by a Met left-hander since Jerry Koosman won 21 in 1976. Koosman, indeed, was 17th to turn the two-league trick, only he did it in reverse, winning 20 for the Twins in 1979. Viola also was among the league leaders in wins, ERA, strikeouts, complete games, winning percentage, and shutouts, and he led the league in innings pitched with 249⅔. He was the hottest thing in the majors at the start of the season, winning his first seven decisions, including a 4-0 April. He started the year with a 17⅔-inning shutout streak. He threw three shutouts during the season, blanking the Reds on May 2, the Dodgers on May 12, and the Astros on July 3. He also pitched seven complete games, giving him 63 for his career. He has 14 career shutouts. After the 7-0 start, his best stretch of the season was from June 22 to July 8, when he won four in a row, allowing just four runs in 33⅔ innings before the All-Star break. Viola also tossed a scoreless inning in the All-Star game. He won four of five decisions from August 22 to September 15. Remarkably, he made 35 starts in his first full season with the Mets and had decisions in 32 of them. Viola's strong start helped keep the Mets in the race early when Gooden and Cone were struggling. If all of them get off well in 1991, it might help the Mets establish themselves in the race. Strong (and consistent) pitching will be the most necessary ingredient for the club.

Age: 31			Bats: Left					Throws: Left		
	W	L	SV	G	CG	IP	HA	BB	SO	ERA
1990	20	12	0	35	7	249.2	227	60	182	2.67
Career	137	110	0	307	63	2107.2	2077	608	1469	3.70

WALLY WHITEHURST

PITCHER

If there was any bright spot in the middle relief of the Mets' bullpen during 1990 (except for some of the work of part-time starter Bob Ojeda), it was Wally Whitehurst. After two brief stints and a total of nine games in 1989, not a lot was expected of Whitehurst. But he produced consistent middle relief for virtually the entire 1990 season. In his first 12 appearances, he collected two saves and had a 1.37 ERA. He got his first big league save on May 7 in relief of Frank Viola, giving up one hit and no runs in 2⅔ innings. He got his second in relief of Dwight Gooden at Los Angeles on May 21, going three innings and allowing a run on three hits. Whitehurst's longest relief outing of the season resulted in his first major league win on July 5 in Atlanta, when he went 4⅔ innings in what turned out to be a 9-8 Mets' victory. He allowed four hits and three earned runs, walked none, and struck out three. This followed a brief sojourn at Tidewater (June 2 to 12). He started two games for the Tides and had a 1-0 record with a 2.00 ERA after nine innings of work, allowing seven hits and a walk and striking out 10. Whitehurst, who will turn 27 in April, has had a fairly long minor league career, largely as a starter. He has appeared in 120 minor league games—in only one of them as a reliever. Three times he has pitched more than 130 innings in a season. In 38 appearances for the Mets last season he had only 65⅔ innings of work. Being used to more innings, Whitehurst can probably be counted on to handle long middle-relief stints when they become necessary, which they do, even with a starting rotation like that of the Mets.

Age: 27			Bats: Right					Throws: Right	
	W	L	SV	G	CG	IP	HA	BB	SO	ERA
1990	1	0	2	38	0	65.2	63	9	46	3.29
Career	1	1	2	47	0	79.2	80	14	55	3.50

CHARLIE O'BRIEN
CATCHER

The Mets acquired Charlie O'Brien from the Brewers on August 31 in a deal for two players to be named later. The Mets also were to receive one player to be named later. When the clubs got around to naming names, the Mets sent pitchers Kevin Brown and Julio Machado to the Brewers and received pitcher Kevin Carmody from Milwaukee. Only time will tell if any of these guys will mean anything to either team. In the meantime, the one known player, O'Brien, started 20 games as a catcher for the Mets in September and October. He continued to exhibit a fine throwing arm, nipping 11 of 24 would-be base-stealers. For his career, O'Brien has thrown out an average of 39 percent of all potential base-stealers, a fairly high rate. O'Brien also showed some flashes of rather unexpected batting punch with a three-RBI game on September 8 against Philadelphia and another one three days later against the Cardinals. With the Brewers he was primarily used as a backup to B. J. Surhoff, but he may turn out to be more of a front-line player with the Mets, depending upon the health of No. 1 catcher Mackey Sasser. He will also see some service when Sasser gets a day off against a tough left-hander. Of course the amount of playing time O'Brien received could very much depend on the Met's offensive outlook and the philosophy of Manager Bud Harrelson. While Sasser has proven to have a lively bat,he is not as good a defensive catcher as O'Brien. With the Mets claiming to emphasize speed, defense and fundamentals in 1991, O'Brien could prove to be quite valuable.

Age: 30			Bats: Right						Throws: Right		
	G	AB	H	2B	3B	HR	R	RBI	BB	SO	SB	BA
1990	74	213	38	10	2	0	17	20	21	34	0	.178
Career	202	565	118	30	3	8	56	65	54	68	0	.209

MACKEY SASSER
CATCHER

Despite a number of problems, including an ankle injury and the death of his father, Mackey Sasser had his finest season in the major leagues in 1990 and became the Mets No. 1 catcher. A late-season elbow injury to Sasser sent the Mets scrambling for more catching in September (Charlie O'Brien was acquired), but there was no doubt that Sasser had established himself as the top man behind the plate. Oddly, his season started very slowly, with just one hit in his first 22 at-bats (.045). But then he went on a tear, hitting .432 with 19 hits in 44 at-bats over a 17-game stretch to boost his average to .303 by June 5. A brief slump knocked him down to .282, but then he hit safely in 17 of 19 games with 26 hits in 65 at-bats (a .400 pace) to drive his average up to a season-high .336 at the All-Star break. However, on July 8, the day before the break, he severely sprained his right ankle in a collision at home plate while tagging out Atlanta's Jim Presley. He was forced out of that game and missed the first five games after the All-Star interlude. He never really recovered from the sprain, hobbling the rest of the season before being shelved by the elbow problem. As a hitter, Sasser is prone to splurges. In two games against the Braves in July he knocked in seven runs, and in two starts against St. Louis later that month he had six RBIs. On July 29 against the Cardinals he collected his first career grand slam home run. On balance, his season was extremely productive, and the 28-year-old appears to be the Mets' catcher for the foreseeable future.

Age: 28			Bats: Left							Throws: Right	
	G	AB	H	2B	3B	HR	R	RBI	BB	SO	SB	BA
1990	100	270	83	14	0	6	31	41	15	19	0	.307
Career	246	602	176	38	3	8	59	82	28	45	0	.292

KEVIN ELSTER
SHORTSTOP

Kevin Elster may be in the position that Wally Pipp of the New York Yankees found himself in more than 50 years ago. Pipp, you may recall, was the Yankees' first baseman who got injured and was replaced by Lou Gehrig. Pipp never got his job back, as Gehrig played a world-record 2,130 games. Elster may face the same problem in 1991 with the Mets. His 1990 season ended when he underwent surgery on his right shoulder on September 4. The arthroscopic procedure by Dr. James Andrews repaired the torn anterior capsule and labrum at the shoulder. Howard Johnson, sometimes employed at shortstop by manager Davey Johnson, then became the regular at the position. He had actually played short much of August as well, when Elster's shoulder began to bother him severely enough to send him to the bench. Now Johnson is protesting plans to move him into the right-field spot vacated by Darryl Strawberry and is insisting that he would rather be the shortstop. Conventional wisdom, of course, is that it is better to have a heavy hitter in the outfield, where he is less injury-prone than he would be in the infield. Nevertheless, Johnson appears to want to be in the middle of the action at shortstop and is opposing the move to right. If he wins the argument, Elster may be the odd man out. One of Elster's problems is his lack of offensive consistency. He is one of the best fielders in the game at his position but has never shown steady performance at the plate. Last season, he twice had four hits in a game but was batting only .088 after his first 23 games and needed a strong drive to get his average to .224. He did that by hitting .289 over a 49-game stretch through July 5 but then slumped again. Elster went to the bench on August 3 and never returned.

Age: 26		Bats: Right						Throws: Right			
	G	AB	H	2B	3B	HR	R	RBI	BB	SO	SB	BA
1990	92	314	65	20	1	9	36	45	30	54	2	.207
Career	416	1218	267	59	4	28	133	138	102	187	8	.219

TOM HERR
SECOND BASE

In slightly over a month with the team, Tommy Herr had an impact on the future of several Mets. He was re-signed and has been installed as the regular second baseman. That means that Gregg Jefferies will be the third baseman (or another outfielder) and that Howard Johnson will be the shortstop (or an outfielder). With the move of Jefferies to third, after he had just settled in at second, the Mets admitted that he wasn't succeeding at the position. Herr is a professional second baseman and makes a significant contribution to the offense. His only real debit is his age. He will turn 35 in April. He was acquired from the Phillies for a pair of minor leaguers at the trading deadline (August 31) and then started 26 games at second base down the stretch, as the Mets made their futile bid to catch the Pirates. Herr made a smashing debut, with a home run in his first game as a Met and with six hits in his first 13 at-bats. In the first game he also made a superb defensive play, throwing out Matt Williams at the plate to kill a Giants' rally. New York is the fourth club of Herr's career, although most fans identify him with the Cardinals. He was traded to Minnesota 15 games into the 1988 season and then went to the Phillies prior to the 1989 season. Despite having played most of his career on artificial surface, Herr has proved to be a good defensive player on any surface, and playing on grass at Shea Stadium may lengthen his career. Last season he committed only three errors in the last 92 games of the season played for the Phils and then the Mets. As switch-hitter, he is nearly equal from both sides of the plate, hitting one point higher (.274 to .273) right-handed for his career.

Age: 35			Bats: Both						Throws: Right			
	G	AB	H	2B	3B	HR	R	RBI	BB	SO	SB	BA
1990	146	547	143	26	3	5	48	60	50	58	7	.261
Career	1412	5134	1405	246	40	27	653	553	582	556	179	.274

GREGG JEFFERIES
INFIELD

Now established as a major-league hitter, Gregg Jefferies and the Mets must decide where he is going to play. Last season, just when Jefferies appeared to be settling down at second base, he was returned to third as a result of the acquisition of Tom Herr. He started at third for the first time on August 14 against the Dodgers but didn't become permanent there until September, when Herr took over at second. He is expected to be the third baseman in 1991. Jefferies is one of the more dangerous switch-hitters in the league and last season led the National League in doubles with 40. He was also among the league leaders in runs scored and multi-hit games. Much heralded as the minor-league player of the year in 1986 and '87 and as a rookie prospect, Jefferies went through a period of adjustment in 1989 but seemed to find himself as a hitter last season. He hit his career-high 13th homer on July 31, had the fourth four-hit game of his career on September 30, and had a career-best four-RBI game against the Phillies on June 24. He had an 11-game hitting streak (matching his career best) and also a nine-gamer. He had 51 multi-hit games, including 14 with three hits and one with four. This all came after he started off by hitting only .253 in April. Then he hit safely in 20 of his next 23 to go up to .302. But Jefferies still poses some questions for Bud Harrelson. In addition to his position in the field, Harrelson must decide where to place him in the batting order. Nonetheless, Jefferies figures to be one of the better hitters in the league for years to come.

Age: 23		Bats: Both									Throws: Right	
	G	AB	H	2B	3B	HR	R	RBI	BB	SO	SB	BA
1990	153	604	171	40	3	15	96	68	46	40	11	.283
Career	329	1227	340	77	7	33	187	143	93	96	37	.277

HOWARD JOHNSON

INFIELD

Given his choice, Howard Johnson will remain the Mets' shortstop. However, with the vacancy created by the departure of Darryl Strawberry in right field, serious consideration is being given to moving him to that spot. Regardless of where he ends up, Johnson will be one of the mainstays of the Mets' offense. Last season he appeared in seven different slots in the batting order, from leadoff to seventh. He appeared only once in the cleanup spot, but he may be hitting there a lot more often in 1991. After starting 80 games at third base, Johnson was moved to shortstop, where he played most of the final 63 games in which he appeared. He committed just one error over a 52-game stretch prior to September 30, handling 218 chances in that span. He finished the season with 34 stolen bases, which placed him fourth on the Mets' all-time list, and stolen bases may become more of an offensive weapon for the Mets this season than they have been in the past. Johnson finished sixth in the National League in extra-base hits (63) and tied for fourth in doubles (37). His most explosive streak came during a 10-game stretch during which he had 12 hits, including six doubles, six runs scored, seven RBIs, and four stolen bases. He had a career-high five-RBI game against the Cubs on June 13, when he hit a grand slam home run, the fifth of his career. He also hit a leadoff homer on July 17 against the Astros and was one of three Mets to open a game with a homer (Gregg Jefferies and Mark Carreon were the other two). Johnson has now hit 20 or more home runs and stolen 20 or more bases for four straight seasons. That kind of consistency will be critical to the Mets in 1991.

Age: 30			Bats: Both						Throws: Right		
	G	AB	H	2B	3B	HR	R	RBI	BB	SO	SB	BA
1990	154	590	144	37	3	23	89	90	69	100	34	.244
Career	1023	3395	868	172	13	159	516	512	443	692	161	.256

DAVE MAGADAN

FIRST BASE

Though oft-maligned as a fielder, Dave Magadan was perhaps the most pleasant surprise on the Mets last season as he became, if not a new Keith Hernandez, then certainly a better fielder than had been expected. By mid-season Magadan was playing a quietly solid first base and also challenging for the league lead in hitting. At the beginning of the season he was sitting on the bench, and off-season acquisition Mike Marshall was starting at first base. When Marshall developed a series of ailments (some of them perhaps psychological), Magadan took over. He had only 14 starts at first base by June 12. But that day he had a sensational game against the Cubs in Chicago, going four-for-four with a triple, a home run, and three runs scored, a career-high six RBIs. He was the regular at first from then on, and Marshall was eventually traded away. At the season's close Magadan had the second highest batting average in Met history at .328 and finished third in the National League batting race behind Willie McGee (.335) and Eddie Murray (.330). He was also second in the league with a .417 on-base percentage and tied for eighth with 74 walks. This was after a slow start in which he had only five hits in his first 25 at-bats. He also put together a couple of hot streaks, including an 11-game hitting streak (the second best of his career), and he had seven hits in seven at-bats in mid-June, missing the club record by one. After his outburst against the Cubs on June 12, he started 72 of the next 76 games and clinched the role of starting first baseman. Although not a consistent power hitter, Magadan is a distinct asset to the Mets' lineup and seems to have the potential to be a batting champion.

Age: 29		Bats: Left								Throws: Right		
	G	AB	H	2B	3B	HR	R	RBI	BB	SO	SB	BA
1990	144	451	148	28	6	6	74	72	74	55	2	.328
Career	478	1349	411	78	10	14	184	175	208	154	3	.305

TIM TEUFEL

INFIELD

Tim Teufel was extremely displeased two years ago when he was removed from the everyday lineup by manager Davey Johnson to make way for young Gregg Jefferies. Now he is buried even deeper, thanks to Tom Herr's incumbency at second base, which has forced Jefferies to third. Last season Teufel made only 37 starts for the Mets, 17 of them at second base (all before Herr was acquired). He also made his first big league start at third and played seven more games there as well as 12 at first. That appears to be the shape of the future for Teufel: filling in at first behind Dave Magadan, at second behind Herr, and at third behind Jefferies. Since the right-handed Teufel still has a fairly potent bat, he will also serve as a late-inning replacement against self-handed pitching and as a pinch hitter in key situations against lefties. During one span in early August last season, Teufel was used as a pinch hitter three times and hit two home runs (on August 1 and 4). He now has five pinch homers for the Mets, plus one he hit for the Twins. One of his big pinch hits in 1990 came against the Phils on June 24, when he hit a two-run, two-out single to lift the Mets to a 6-5 victory. Teufel had seven multi-hit games during the season, getting three hits three times, and he finished the year with a roar, collecting five hits in his final nine at-bats, including two home runs and a pair of doubles. His hottest streak, though, came between August 18 and September 4, when he appeared in 11 games and hit safely in 10 of them.

Age: 32				Bats: Right					Throws: Right			
	G	AB	H	2B	3B	HR	R	RBI	BB	SO	SB	BA
1990	80	175	43	11	0	10	28	24	15	33	0	.246
Career	759	2325	610	148	10	61	325	279	278	370	10	.262

DARYL BOSTON

CENTER FIELD

After playing 500 major-league games with the Chicago White Sox, Daryl Boston became the prize pickup of the 1990 Mets. He was acquired on a waiver claim on April 30 after being in only five games for the Sox. For the Mets, he proved to be a powerful addition, starting 90 games in center field for a club that needed help at the position. Boston started primarily against right-handed pitching and got off to a quick start, hitting .313 with 20 hits in his first 64 at-bats in New York. He finished the season with a career-high 45 RBIs. Now only 28, he could have several productive years ahead of him if he makes a full recovery from the shoulder separation that prematurely ended his season on September 30, when he made a diving attempt at a ball hit by the Cubs' Ryne Sandberg. Despite a batting style in which he releases his top hand on the follow-through, Boston showed some power, a commodity that is expected to be in somewhat shorter supply for the Mets this season thanks to the departure of Darryl Strawberry to the Dodgers. After making his major league debut in 1984, Boston shuttled between the White Sox and the minor leagues until 1987, when he played his first full season at Comiskey Park. In 1984, he had probably his finest minor league season, batting .312 at Denver with 40 stolen bases in 127 games, and was named as one of the top 10 prospects in the American Association. He also had 19 triples, the most in the league for almost 20 years. His speed is an asset he tends to use more in the outfield than on the bases, but he may be encouraged to run more this season as the Mets seek to compensate for the decline of power.

Age: 28			Bats: Left							Throws: Left		
	G	AB	H	2B	3B	HR	R	RBI	BB	SO	SB	BA
1990	120	367	100	21	2	12	65	45	28	50	19	.273
Career	615	1717	423	84	15	50	244	168	137	290	70	.246

MARK CARREON

OUTFIELD

A potential power bat for the Mets, Mark Carreon had a peculiar season in 1990. He experienced his finest major league season, hitting a career-high 10 home runs and driving in a career-high 26 RBIs with a .250 batting average in 82 games, principally against left-handed pitching. He also delivered several key pinch hits for the Mets. However, his season was cut short by a knee knjury suffered while running the bases at San Diego on August 21. He tore the anterior cruciate ligament in his right knee while rounding third base and missed the remainder of the season. The knee was operated on four days after the injury. In the closing days of the season, it was revealed that Carreon had entered a New York rehabilitation center for treatment of alcohol abuse, thus further clouding his future. If he is fully recovered from the knee surgery and the drinking problem, Carreon could be a major factor for the Mets in 1991. He is only one pinch-hit home run short of the club record of six shared by Rusty Staub and Ed Kranepool. He delivered a key pinch homer, the fifth of his Met career, on June 13 against the Cubs in the ninth inning of the second game of a doubleheader at Wrigley Field. He might see more regular action in the outfield this season if he is healthy. Last season he started 10 games in left field, and in one of them, on June 17 at Pittsburgh, he had the first two-home-run game of his career. He also started 26 games in center field and five games in right field.

Age: 27			Bats: Right						Throws: Left		
	G	AB	H	2B	3B	HR	R	RBI	BB	SO	SB	BA
1990	82	188	47	12	0	10	30	26	15	29	1	.250
Career	166	342	96	20	0	17	55	44	30	48	3	.281

KEVIN McREYNOLDS

OUTFIELD

Although this taciturn outfielder seems to be the Met the New York media loves to hate, Kevin McReynolds is perhaps the finest fundamental player on the Mets, and one of the best in the National League. He had his fourth straight 20-plus home-run season last year and will loom large in the club's plans this season. If healthy, McReynolds will be a key ingredient as the Mets structure their club in the post-Strawberry era. As an outfielder, he is superb in his ability to position himself for throws. He tied for the NL lead in outfield assists last season (14) and has accumulated 50 assists over the last four seasons, an extraordinary performance for a left fielder. He delivered several game-winning hits for the Mets last season, including a three-run 11th-inning homer in the first game of a doubleheader against Houston and an eighth-inning homer in the second game that was also the game-winner. He had another game-winning homer in the ninth inning on August 24 to give the Mets a 3-2 win at Los Angeles. He drove in 11 runs in 10 games between June 5 and 13. He hit his fifth career grand slam on May 21 and now has three of the Mets' last seven grand slams. After being acquired by the Mets from the Padres in December 1986, McReynolds was generally used as a fifth-place hitter to back up Strawberry. This season either McReynolds or Johnson will be moved to the fourth spot with Howard Johnson hitting ahead of him. The Mets potential for run-production has been diminished by the departure of their leading home-run hitter and RBI producer, so McReynolds's output will become all the more important to the club.

Age: 31			Bats: Right							Throws: Right	
	G	AB	H	2B	3B	HR	R	RBI	BB	SO	SB	BA
1990	147	521	140	23	1	24	75	82	71	61	9	.269
Career	1089	3997	1080	194	28	167	550	621	349	523	76	.270

KEITH MILLER

OUTFIELD

As the Opening Day center fielder for the Mets in 1990, Keith Miller may eventually fall in the same category as Bob Lemon. Lemon, later famous as a 200-game winner for the Indians, was the Opening Day center fielder for Cleveland in 1946—but quickly found that his baseball future lay elsewhere. One of the questions facing Keith Miller is where *his* future might lie. He had a difficult time in center field after being shifted there when the Mets ran out of candidates. His previous experience had been almost entirely as an infielder, a fact that rapidly became obvious. Miller, however, is an intense, hard-working player who makes the most of his talent. He is likely to wind up as a swing man and backup for whatever outfield alignment emerges for the Mets this spring. Last year was further complicated for him by two separate stints on the disabled list resulting from a mild hamstring pull in late April and a lower-back strain in August. When he did play, Miller appeared as the handyman, playing six different positions: three in the outfield and second, short, and third. He made 42 starts in center field, mostly against left-handed pitching after the end of April, when the Mets signed Daryl Boston. Miller did have four three-hit games and at one point had 14 straight stolen bases before being picked off on August 5 at St. Louis. He started the season with his most consistent batting stretch of the year, hitting .283 with 13 hits in 46 at-bats over a 12-game period in April. But then he was in and out of the lineup the rest of the way, used often as a pinch hitter and shuffled around from one position to another. He can expect more of the same this season.

Age: 27			Bats: Right						Throws: Right			
	G	AB	H	2B	3B	HR	R	RBI	BB	SO	SB	BA
1990	88	233	60	8	0	1	42	12	23	46	16	.258
Career	210	497	127	18	3	3	80	25	36	89	30	.256

VINCE COLEMAN
OUTFIELD

In his six seasons with the St. Louis Cardinals, Vince Coleman established himself as one of the outstanding base stealers in baseball history. As a rookie in 1985, Coleman led the majors with 110 steals, setting a modern rookie record in the process. Although he has never matched that total, Coleman has led the NL in stolen bases every year that he has played. He also has a fairly high ratio of successful steals: 83%. Last season he stole 77 bases in 94 attempts (82%). His 1990 season was perhaps his best all-around. He had a career-high .292 batting average in 124 games with the Cardinals and also hit a career-best six home runs—although no one takes him seriously as a long-ball threat. (He has only 15 home runs in 878 major league games.) He also had his best-ever slugging (.400) and on-base (.340) percentages in 1990, despite missing nearly 40 games with injuries. Coleman first captured serious baseball attention during his second season in the minor leagues (1983), when he destroyed the South Atlantic League, stealing 143 bases in 113 games and also winning the league's batting championship with a .350 average. Counting his three years in the minors, Coleman has never played a full season in any league and not led that league in steals. Although he is considered by some to be defensively weak and does not have a good throwing arm, Coleman brings a very explosive offensive force to his team, and the Mets are hoping that he will enable them to make up for some of the lost run-production created by the departure of Darryl Strawberry.

Age: 30				Bats: Both						Throws: Right		
	G	AB	H	2B	3B	HR	R	RBI	BB	SO	SB	AVG.
1990	124	497	145	18	9	6	73	39	35	88	77	.292
Career	878	3535	937	106	56	15	566	217	314	628	549	.265

1990 SEASON

While the Mets finished second in the National League East in 1990, everyone connected with the organization would no doubt classify the season as a failure.

This, of course, is part of the price of high expectations, and what the Mets (and their fans) expected in 1990 was another pennant. Or at least a division title.

With a pitching staff of Dwight Gooden, Frank Viola, Sid Fernandez, Ron Darling, Bob Ojeda, and David Cone, and with John Franco in the bullpen, New York had the best arms in the league.

But pennants aren't won on the drawing board, they are won on the field, and that pitching staff didn't live up to expectations.

Gooden started slowly but then hit his stride and was the club's most consistent pitcher during the second half of the season, winning 16 of 17 decisions after starting 3-5 (although he lost his change at a 20-win season in the final week at Pittsburgh).

Viola and Franco, on the other hand, both started very well. Viola led the league in wins at the All-Star break but then struggled and failed four times in September to get his 20th victory. Franco experienced a similar late fade, although he wound up leading the league in saves.

Indeed, it was supremely ironic that the Mets were eliminated in their final home game of the season and that Franco allowed four runs in the final two innings to turn a 5-2 lead over the Cubs into a 6-5 defeat, while the Pirates were winning in St. Louis.

Here was a team that struggled both early and late in the season.

After a 20-22 start, the front office decided it was the fault of the manager, Davey Johnson (the winningest field boss in the club's history), so they dismissed him. Johnson had managed over 1,000 games for the Mets and had brought them through the world championship in 1986 and to a division title two years later.

But in 1990 he was no longer the answer. Bud Harrelson, the shortstop on the Mets' 1969 world champs, got the call. After a slow beginning, the Mets went on their one major move of the season, winning 26 of 31 games before the All-Star break.

New York was the hottest team in the majors at that point and managed to remain in first place briefly into August. They regained the top spot, again briefly, in early September.

But September was easily the cruelest month for the Mets, who lost 12 of their first 19 games and began to slip back, as Pittsburgh moved to the top of the division. When the Pirates hit a skid and lost six in a row from September 12 through September 18, the Mets made up three games — but only played .500 (3-3) and never really mounted a serious drive.

Overall, the Mets were around .500 for the season if the one hot streak (26-5) is excluded from their final record.

What hurt the most was their inability to win consistently against left-handed pitching and their inability to win close games. These are two things that championship teams must do. New York, however, was a miserable 25-31 against lefty starters and 32-41 in games decided by two runs or less. This came about despite the fact that the Mets led the National League in both home runs and runs scored.

Perhaps one of the problems was the prolonged absence of shortstop Kevin Elster, whose shoulder problems forced him to the sidelines for good in August. Whether he will return and in what condition remains one of the questions the Mets will have to face in 1991.

Elster's absence led to a general reshuffling of the infield defense. Third baseman Howard Johnson was moved to short, and second baseman Gregg Jefferies eventually wound up at second, a move solidified after the trading-deadline acquisition of veteran second baseman Tommy Herr.

In the early going Johnson played off-season purchase Mike Marshall as the regular at first base. The manager suggested that this was a requirement by the front office. After Johnson left, however, a minor injury shelved Marshall, and Dave Magadan returned to first.

Magadan was one of the highlights of the season. He emerged during the course of the summer as a serious contender for the NL batting title and hit .328 for the year. Magadan also developed into a more-than-adequate defensive first baseman, somewhat to the chagrin of his detractors.

But all the movement had a price. The lack of infield cohesion was perhaps one of the explanations for the Mets' poor showing in close games. On a couple of occasions in September the club failed to turn a double play, and the opposition used the extra out to score. One key game against Chicago was lost in just this fashion.

Pitching is, of course, connected directly to defense, and the foundering of the pitching staff may, in part, be traced to the state of flux in the infield.

One of the pleasant surprises for the Mets was the play of center fielder Daryl Boston. When the season began, it appeared that center field would be a problem. Again, Johnson pointed the finger at the front office when questioned about infielder Keith Miller being stationed as the regular in center.

After Harrelson took over, Miller wound up on the bench and was replaced by Boston, who had been released by the White Sox, for whom he had had played over 500 games.

Boston became the regular, impressing both on defense and at the plate. He hit .273 for the season with 12 homers and 45 RBIs despite his late start. In the field, he was superb. In fact, his season was cut three games short when he suffered a separated shoulder while making a spectacular catch, robbing Ryne Sandberg of a probable three-base hit.

Still, many wonder if Boston can repeat his performance offensively now that the NL pitchers have had a season to study him. In partial answer to this, Boston did hit .310 over his final 10 games after having batted over 350 times against the league.

At the close of the season, there was much confusion in the ranks at Shea Stadium. Darryl Strawberry, the club's all-time leading home-run and RBI producer, was declaring himself a free agent. Strawberry said he might like to play in Los Angeles, where he was raised and where his wife and children reside.

To make matters worse, the front office man most involved in player personnel — Joe McIlvaine — left. He left to become the general manager of the San Diego Padres at a time when his boss, general manager Frank Cashen, was supposedly preparing to retire. Cashen subsequently agreed to a two-year deal to remain in charge.

Worse, perhaps, was the fact that the highly regarded McIlvaine's move became public during the closing stretches of the pennant race and so became another distraction for a team that already had plenty to contend with.

Late-season injuries to Strawberry (back) and left fielder Kevin McReynolds (toe) also crippled the offense in the closing days of the race, although neither was serious enough to cause worry about the players' futures.

McIlvaine, on the other hand, is gone at a time when the Mets' farm system will need some rebuilding. Many young prospects had been traded away to obtain help for the immediate future — such as Herr, and catcher Charlie O'Brien, who was acquired from Milwaukee when Mackey Sasser was injured.

But when all is said and done, at the beginning of the 1990 season the Mets certainly looked like a team that had the talent to win the division, if not the pennant.

They were undermined by inconsistent performance. Fernandez, for instance, did not win a game in September despite his usual low opponent batting average and high strikeout totals. He finished with a 9-14 record despite a 3.46 ERA in 29 starts. He struck out 181 men in 179 1/3 innings.

Met pitchers led the league in strikeouts, and Cone led the Mets pitchers with 233 in 211 2/3 innings but was only 14-10 thanks to a slow start. He at least finished up strongly, striking out 12 while pitching a three-hitter and driving in two runs himself in a 4-1 win over Pittsburgh in his final start.

Unfortunately, Cone's strong finish was not shared by his team.

Frank Viola

HISTORY

One of the odd things about the New York Mets is that their creation was brought about by men who never had any interest, financial or otherwise, in the team.

After the New York Giants and Brooklyn Dodgers moved to the West Coast following the 1957 season, the absence of the National League in New York City prompted several actions.

With New York as a potential franchise site, several wealthy sportsmen, including Jack Kent Cook, formed a new league (called the Continental League) and hired Branch Rickey, former general manager of the St. Louis Cardinals, Brooklyn Dodgers, and Pittsburgh Pirates, to head it.

Meanwhile, others in New York formed a committee to help bring an NL team to New York. Included in this group were its leader, lawyer William A. Shea, wealthy department store owner Bernard Gimble, and real estate investor Clinton W. Blume, a one-time pitcher with the New York Giants (1922–23).

These two groups, working in opposite directions, forced the first expansion of modern baseball and pushed the National League into granting a franchise to New York. Mrs. Charles Shipman Payson, an heir to the Whitney fortune and a former minority shareholder in the New York Giants, backed the syndicate that bought the expansion team.

Several sportswriters campaigned to have the team called "the Mets," partly because the first major league team in New York in 1883 was known by that name. In fact, when the first authorized

World Series was played, in 1884, the Mets represented the American Association against the Providence Grays of the National League. Perhaps as an augury, the Grays swept the Series in three straight games. By the late 1880s, the Mets were gone, and in 1891 the American Association sank from sight. But the tradition lingered on in New York baseball lore.

Mrs. Payson liked the idea, and the corporate name of the new team became the Metropolitan Baseball Club; nickname: the Mets.

Mrs. Payson hired two famous ex-Yankees to run the team: general manager (and club president) George M. Weiss and field manager Casey Stengel.

Fortunately, the new team touched the loyalties of former NL fans in New York—because its on-the-field performance was truly something to behold.

In its first year, 1962, the team featured a collection of largely over-the-hill players and a smattering of rookies. The poor quality of play became the stuff of which legends are made.

Several times during the season it seemed that weeks passed without the team winning. At season's end, the new team had won 40 games, lost 120, and finished a staggering 60½ games out of first place.

During their early years, the Mets were perennial tail-enders. Five times in their first six seasons the Mets lost over 100 games. But Stengel's antics kept fans and writers alike amused, and a whole coterie of fans, called "the New Breed," grew up around the Mets, making them almost a cult object.

In 1964 the Mets moved from the historic but

aging Polo Grounds into Shea Stadium, located in Queens, across the street from the World's Fair that opened that spring. Attendance soared to 1,732,597.

But the futile performance on the field continued. Then in 1967 the Mets acquired Gil Hodges (one of their original players five years before) as manager. Their 1968 record of 73-89 was the best in team history up to that point.

In 1969 a remarkable thing happened. The Mets won the pennant. Then an even more remarkable thing happened. The Mets won the World Series, defeating the Baltimore Orioles in five games.

As stunning as man's arrival on the moon earlier that year, the Mets' victory brought forth a massive celebration in New York, with City Hall receptions and ticker-tape parades down Broadway for Hodges and his players, including Cleon Jones, Tom Seaver, Jerry Koosman, Nolan Ryan, and Bud Harrelson.

After two third-place finishes, the Mets appeared poised to make another pennant run in 1972 when a heart attack struck down manager Gil Hodges during spring training. Yogi Berra, a former Yankee star and then a Met coach, was named to replace the late Hodges.

Under Berra the Mets produced another, albeit smaller, miracle in 1973 by winning the NL East and surprising Cincinnati's Big Red Machine in the playoffs, three games to two. New York led the World Series against Oakland three games to two, but the A's won the final two games in Oakland.

Then came a decade of decline. Although attendance remained high for several seasons, the team was not a serious contender. Finally, the attendance also began to drop. Mrs. Payson died after the 1975 season, and her heirs decided to sell the club in 1980 to a syndicate headed by publisher Nelson Doubleday.

After a series of managerial changes, Davey Johnson took the helm in 1984, and the Mets immediately became a contender again. In his first six seasons, Johnson never had a team finish lower than second. In 1986 and 1988 the Mets won the NL East.

In 1986 the Mets defeated the Houston Astros in a wild six-game series for the pennant, and then rallied from being one strike away from elimination in Game 6 to win the World Series from the Boston Red Sox in seven games.

In 1988 the Mets lost their bid to return to the Series when the Los Angeles Dodgers won the championship series, four games to three.

Casey Stengel

Despite another second-place finish the following season, Johnson was on thin ice in 1990. And when the team started 20-22, he was dismissed. Former Met hero Bud Harrelson, shortstop for the team's first two pennant-winning teams, was the new manager.

During the 1980s the Mets developed a cadre of stars, including pitcher Dwight (Doc) Gooden, who became the youngest pitcher ever to win 100 games, slugging outfielder Darryl Strawberry, and switch-hitting third baseman Howard Johnson.

This cast was augmented by the acquisition of such older stars as first baseman Keith Hernandez (from St. Louis), catcher Gary Carter (from Montreal), and outfielder Kevin McReynolds (from San Diego).

Moving into the 1990s the Mets added some younger players, like shortstop Kevin Elster, second baseman Gregg Jefferies, and Dave Magadan, Hernandez's successor at first base.

At the start of 1990 the Mets remained the only NL expansion team ever to win a World Series—and they had done it twice.

The Mets Walk On the Moon!: The NY Mets and Jerry Koosman beat Baltimore 3–1 in the fifth and final game of the World Series and win their first world championship (October 16, 1969)

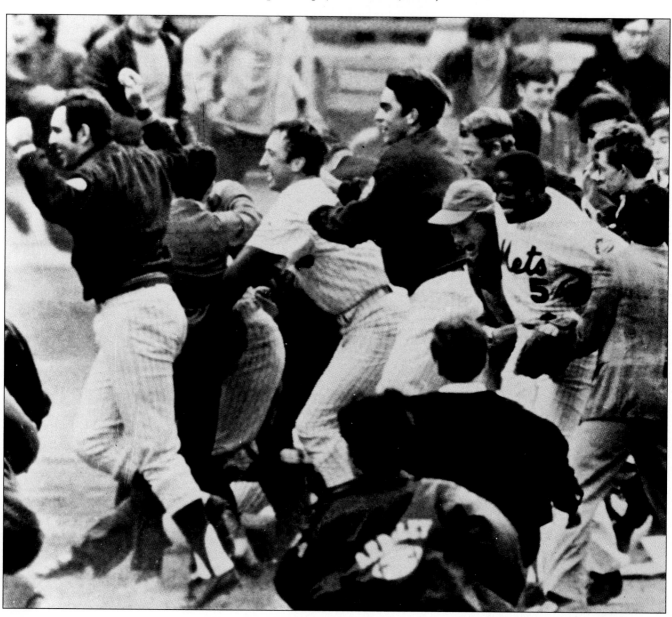

1990 TEAM LEADERS

BATTING

Darryl Strawberry

Games .... Howard Johnson	154
At-bats .... Gregg Jefferies	604
Batting average .... Dave Magadan	.328
Runs .... Gregg Jefferies	96
Hits .... Gregg Jefferies	171
Doubles .... Gregg Jefferies	40
Triples .... Dave Magadan	6
Home runs .... Darryl Strawberry	37
On-base percentage ..... Dave Magadan	.417
Slugging percentage . Darryl Strawberry	.518
RBIs .... Darryl Strawberry	108
Total bases .... Darryl Strawberry	281
Walks .... Dave Magadan	74
Most strikeouts .... Darryl Strawberry	110
Stolen bases .... Howard Johnson	34
Caught stealing .... Darryl Strawberry	8

1990 TEAM LEADERS

PITCHING

Dwight Gooden

Games	John Franco	55
Wins	Frank Viola	20
Losses	Sid Fernandez	14
Starts	Frank Viola	35
Complete games	Frank Viola	7
Shutouts	Frank Viola	3
Innings	Frank Viola	249 ⅔
ERA	Frank Viola	2.67
Strikeouts	David Cone	233
Walks	Sid Fernandez	67
Saves	John Franco	33
Relief appearances	John Franco	55
Winning percentage	Frank Viola	.625
Hits allowed	Dwight Gooden	229

1990 TRANSACTIONS

DATE	PLAYER	TRANSACTION
March 29	Terry Bross	Sent to minor league camp for reassignment
	Kevin Brown	Sent to minor league camp for reassignment
	Mike Miller	Sent to minor league camp for reassignment
	Pete Schourek	Sent to minor league camp for reassignment
	Dave Trautwein	Sent to minor league camp for reassignment
	Julio Valera	Sent to minor league camp for reassignment
	Todd Hundley	Sent to minor league camp for reassignment
	Chris Donnels	Sent to minor league camp for reassignment
	Terry McDaniel	Sent to minor league camp for reassignment
	Jaime Roseboro	Sent to minor league camp for reassignment
April 5	Brent Knackert	Claimed on waivers by Seattle
	Phil Lombardi	Claimed on waivers by Atlanta
April 6	Blaine Beatty	Placed on 60-day emergency disabled list (left elbow surgery)
April 7	Orlando Mercado	Purchased from Tidewater
April 8	Keith Hughes	Outrighted to Tidewater
April 25	Jeff Innis	Optioned to Tidewater
	Chuck Carr	Purchased from Jackson
April 30	Keith Miller	Placed on 15-day disabled list (retroactive to April 25; right hamstring)
	Darren Reed	Purchased from Tidewater
	Daryl Boston	Claimed on waivers from White Sox
	Orlando Mercado	Outrighted to Tidewater
	Lou Thornton	Optioned to Tidewater
	Chuck Carr	Optioned to Jackson
May 6	Darren Reed	Optioned to Tidewater
May 17	Keith Miller	Reinstated from disabled list
May 18	Barry Lyons	Placed on 15-day disabled list (retroactive to May 16; lower back)
	Todd Hundley	Recalled from Jackson
May 30	Lou Thornton	Recalled and outrighted to Tidewater
	Todd Hundley	Optioned to Jackson
June 1	Orlando Mercado	Purchased from Tidewater
June 2	Wally Whitehurst	Optioned to Tidewater
June 3	Dave Liddell	Purchased from Tidewater
June 12	Dave Liddell	Optioned to Tidewater
June 13	Wally Whitehurst	Recalled from Tidewater
June 17	Jeff Innis	Recalled from Tidewater
June 18	Julio Machado	Optioned to Tidewater
	Dave Liddell	Recalled and outrighted to Tidewater
June 19	Barry Lyons	Assigned to Tidewater under terms of Major League Rehabilitation Program
July 9	Barry Lyons	Optioned to Tidewater
July 11	Jeff Musselman	Optioned to Tidewater
July 12	Todd Hundley	Recalled from Jackson
July 16	Mike Marshall	Placed on 15-day disabled list (retroactive to July 13; duodenitis)
	Mario Diaz	Recalled from Tidewater
July 20	Jaime Roseboro	Recalled (not to report) and outrighted to Jackson
July 22	Jeff Innis	Optioned to Tidewater
July 23	Julio Machado	Recalled from Tidewater
July 25	Todd Hundley	Optioned to Jackson
July 26	Kevin Brown	Recalled from Tidewater

DATE	PLAYER	TRANSACTION
July 28	Mike Marshall	Reinstated from disabled list and traded to Boston Red Sox for RHP Greg Hansell, OF Ender Perozo and PTBNL (not charged to 40-man roster)
August 2	Kevin Brown	Optioned to Tidewater
August 3	Alex Trevino	Signed as free agent
August 4	Kevin Elster	Placed on 15-day disabled list (tendinitis, right shoulder)
August 7	Kelvin Torve	Purchased from Tidewater
August 15	Keith Miller	Placed on 15-day disabled list (lower back spasms)
August 16	Darren Reed	Recalled from Tidewater
August 21	Mark Carreon	Placed on 15-day disabled list (torn ligament, right knee)
	Chuck Carr	Recalled from Tidewater
August 24	Mark Carreon	Transferred to 60-day disabled list
August 24	Julio Machado	Optioned to Tidewater
August 25	Todd Hundley	Recalled from Jackson
August 28	Mario Diaz	Optioned to Tidewater
August 29	Kevin Baez	Purchased from Jackson
August 30	Pat Tabler	Acquired from Kansas City for RHP Archie Corbin
	Orlando Mercado	Claimed by Montreal under MLR 10
	Julio Valera	Recalled from Tidewater
	Chuck Carr	Optioned to Jackson
August 31	Tom Herr	Acquired from Philadelphia for RHP Rockey Elli and IF Nikco Riesgo
	Charlie O'Brien	Acquired from Milwaukee with PTBNL for 2 PTBNL
	Alex Trevino	Placed on waivers for the purpose of his unconditional release
	Kevin Elster	Transferred to 60-day the disabled list
	Kelvin Torve	Optioned to Tidewater
September 1	Keith Miller	Reinstated from the disabled list
September 2	Kevin Brown	Recalled from Tidewater
September 4	Julio Machado	Recalled from Tidewater
	Jeff Musselman	Recalled from Tidewater
	Jeff Innis	Recalled from Tidewater
	Kelvin Torve	Recalled from Tidewater
	Chris Jelic	Purchased from Tidewater
	Barry Lyons	Placed on waivers for unconditional release
September 7	Alex Trevino	Claimed by Cincinnati under MLR 10
	Kevin Brown	Sent to Milwaukee to complete O'Brien deal
	Julio Machado	Sent to Milwaukee to complete O'Brien deal
	Keith Hughes	Purchased from Tidewater
	Terrance Bross	Recalled from Jackson; not to report
	Mike Miller	Recalled from Jackson; not to report
	Chris Donnels	Recalled from Jackson; not to report
	Chuck Carr	Recalled from Jackson; not to report
	Terry McDaniel	Recalled from Jackson; not to report
September 10	Dan Schatzeder	Acquired from Houston for RHP Steve LaRose and IF Nickey Davis
	Peter Schourek	Recalled from Port St. Lucie; not to report
September 12	Mario Diaz	Recalled from Tidewater; not to report
	David Trautwein	Recalled from Tidewater; not to report

1991 ASSESSMENT

One of the most telling observations about the New York Mets was made by former player-personnel boss Joe McIlvaine, who said, "The Mets have the best club on paper every year, and look what happens."

Last season the Mets were 75-55 after 130 games and were in first place on September 1. However, they split their next 28 games evenly and wound up being eliminated before they even got to Pittsburgh for the final three games of the year. After the All-Star break, the Mets were 42-38, hardly a championship-caliber performance.

Pittsburgh, which hardly seemed a team to match up with the Mets, won the division by four games.

All this came about despite a managerial change in late May that put former Met shortstop and hero Bud Harrelson at the helm in place of Davey Johnson. Johnson, despite his critics, was one of the winningest managers in baseball history and guided the Mets both to the 1986 World Championship and to the 1988 East division title.

One of the interesting cases on the Mets, for instance, is left-hander Sid Fernandez. Twice in the last three seasons he has held opposing hitters to the lowest batting average allowed by any pitcher in the league. Yet he has never been a consistent winner. Indeed, last season he was 9-14.

And New York's disappointing finish last season came despite the fact that Darryl Strawberry set a club record for RBIs for a single season (108), David Cone led the NL in strikeouts (233), Fernandez had the lowest opponent batting average, Dave Mag-adan finished third in the batting race with a .328 average, and Frank Viola won 20 games.

It boggles the mind that a team can achieve all of these individual milestones, and yet not add up to a winner. In New York the conventional wisdom among the pundits of the press box is that the team lacks "spirit" and "intensity."

Looking over the Mets' lineup, it really is hard to fathom why they don't win more often. Shifting Howard Johnson to shortstop after Kevin Elster's shoulder went out last year gave the Mets more firepower, but it may have cost them ever so slightly in the field. Nonetheless, it is likely Johnson will be at shortstop again this season.

It now seems clear, too, that Tom Herr is going to be the second baseman. This moves Gregg Jefferies back to third and seems to confine Tim Teufel to the bench.

It is, frankly, difficult to imagine that the team will get the maximum performance from as many players this season as it did last season. And this time around, the Mets will be without their most impressive hitter, Strawberry, who moved to the Dodgers during the off-season after acrimonious free-agent negotiations with the Mets.

Filling the hole left by Strawberry's big bat will be one of the major challenges facing Harrelson as he starts his first full season as the Mets' manager. A continued strong performance by the pitching staff, including Dwight Gooden (19-7 last season), and a tighter defensive performance will be essential if the Mets are even to retain the No. 2 spot in the division this season.

PROSPECTS

ANTHONY YOUNG
Pitcher

To some observers the emergence of Anthony Young as a top pitcher at the double-A level was something of a surprise. But his 9-6 record in A ball in 1989 was misleading, because his season had been ended prematurely by an ankle fracture on July 19.

However, his performance at Jackson in the Texas League in 1990 left little doubt as to his potential. He was 15-3 with a 1.65 ERA in 23 starts. This right-handed pitcher is not quite the hard thrower that his 6'2" 200-pound frame would indicate, but he has good control and excellent movement on his pitches. He walked only 52 men in 158 innings in 1990 at Jackson while striking out 95 and allowing only 116 hits.

While he will probably start the 1991 season at Tidewater, Young does have a chance to make the Mets in spring training and at the very least will be rated as the top pitching prospect in the organization.

If he does not earn a spot on the Mets staff in 1991, Young figures to be one of the early call-ups if the big-league club runs into trouble during the season.

One of the problems he faces, of course, is that the Mets went through the 1990 season with a surplus of starting pitching. However, if Young begins well, he may present the parent club with a few options with respect to dealing off some of that surplus pitching.

DARREN REED
Outfield

As one of the prospects obtained by the Mets in their trade of shortstop Rafael Santana to the Yankees in 1987, Reed has been slowly reaching the potential predicted for him when he batted .500 as a senior All-State catcher in California.

Reed was also a Junior College All-America choice at Ventura J.C. (Calif.), where he hit .486 before signing with the Yankees. The Yanks converted him to an outfielder in 1984 at the A level. He was something of a disappointment until he batted .319 with 20 homers at Albany (double-A) in 1987 and then was swapped to the Mets.

In 1990, his third season at triple-A with Tidewater, he finally seemed to come of age as a hitter, batting .265 with 44 extra-base hits and 74 RBIs in 104 games before being called up for a September look-see by the Mets.

During his stretch with the parent club, Reed batted only .205 but showed considerable punch. His eight hits included six for extra-bases (four doubles, a triple and a homer).

Reed was originally shifted to the outfield because the Yankees felt that he had enough speed to play somewhere besides catcher. In 1990, he was second on the Tidewater squad in stolen bases.

Depending upon how the Mets' outfield shapes up in 1991, Reed has a chance to be a major leaguer this season.

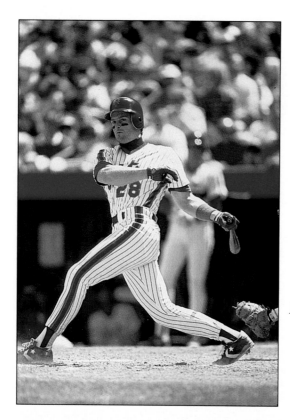

Darren Reed

D.J. Dozier

TERRY BROSS
Relief Pitcher

A former center and forward on St. John's Big East basketball team, Terry Bross had become the premier relief pitching prospect in the Mets' system.

His baseball development was probably retarded by his basketball experience, since he played just one season of baseball at St. John's and pitched only 21 innings. During his first two seasons at the A level, Bross had only one save, although he did spend some time as a starter before being moved exclusively to the bullpen.

However, in 1990, this 6'9" 230-pounder emerged as the dominant reliever in double-A for Jackson, collecting 28 saves in 57 appearances (he finished 47 of those games). He allowed only 42 hits in just under 70 innings as the team's closer.

The entire rest of the bullpen for Jackson totalled only 14 saves.

With John Franco as the primary reliever for the Mets, Bross will not be expected to serve as a closer if he makes the varsity this spring. But his ability to serve that role might take some of the pressure off Franco.

On the other hand, he can serve a very valuable purpose as the main set-up man for Franco if the Mets believe that he is ready to face major league hitters on a regular basis. He is a distinct possibility to make the club since one of the softest parts of the Mets' armor last season was the middle relief which frequently allowed games to get away before Franco could come on to save them.

OTHER MET PROSPECTS TO WATCH

D.J. Dozier is primarily known to sports fans as a Penn State All-American football player, but the Mets rate him a top outfield prospect. As a result, the Mets have encouraged him to concentrate on baseball. At Port St. Lucie in 1990, Dozier made only two errors in 71 games as an outfielder. Overall, he played 106 games and produced a .297 batting average. He was second on the team in homers (13), third in RBIs (57) and third in stolen bases (33) in his first year of professional baseball.

Pete Schourek is a left-handed pitcher who appears headed for the Mets, perhaps as early as 1991. In 1990 he moved from double-A to triple-A late in the season and won one of his two starts at Tidewater. The other was a no-decision. He earned his promotion after a superb season at double-A in which he was 11-4 at Jackson with a 3.04 ERA and 94 strikeouts in 124 innings.

Chris Donnels is a third baseman who was the Mets' first choice in the 1987 June amateur draft and the 24th player chosen overall in the nation. Donnels was all-league three times in college at Loyola Marymount, batting .389, .350, and .365 with 37 homers and 166 RBIs in his three seasons. But he had an uneven beginning to his pro career. After two slow seasons, Donnels began to show his potential, becoming MVP of the Florida State League in 1989 after he hit .313 with 17 homers and a league-leading 78 RBIs. In 1990 he hit .274 in 128 games with 12 homers at double-A Jackson.

Todd Hundley, son of long-time Cub catcher Randy Hundley, caught several games as a starter for the Mets in 1990 but still must be classified as a prospect. A switch-hitter, Hundley was called up when an emergency developed in the Mets' catching corps. At Jackson (double-A) he hit .265 in 85 games.

KEY TRANSACTIONS

One could perhaps say that the most important transaction in the history of the New York Mets was the 1962 expansion draft. It was this "transaction" that began the real history of the Mets because it stocked the team with its first allotment of players.

They were now more than a piece of paper, more than a franchise, more than an idea. They were now a baseball team with real players.

Of course, how real some of those players were is open to question. Three of the original expansion Mets were catchers, and when manager Casey Stengel was asked about this, he replied, "Because you have to have a catcher. Without one, you get a lot of passed balls."

That line, naturally, was a joke. But, perhaps, so too were the original expansion Mets, who won only 40 games during their first season. One of the better players that year was veteran center fielder Richie Ashburn, who batted .306. However, after enduring a season with the Mets, he decided to retire and took up broadcasting for the Phillies.

Another of the original expansion Mets was Frank Thomas, a strong right-handed pull hitter who took advantage of the cozy confines of the Polo Grounds in left field and hit 34 home runs. That stood as a club record until 1975—which gives you some idea of how few power hitters the Mets have had during their history.

One of the most important single acquisitions ever made by the Mets came about through the luck of the draw. When the commissioner ruled that a young pitcher from Southern California had been illegally signed by the Braves in 1966, three teams asked for the right to bid for him. The commissioner, William Eckert, drew the name of the winning team out of the hat. The winning team was the Mets. The pitcher was Tom Seaver.

Seaver, who was to win 311 games in his major league career, was the mainstay of the Mets' pennant winners in 1969 and 1973 and was so important to the team that the local press in New York frequently referred to him as "the Franchise."

Two other key acquisitions that led to the Mets' 1969 championship were the 1967 trade that sent pitcher Bill Dennehy (and $100,000) to the Washington Senators for Gil Hodges, who became the manager of the Mets, and the 1969 deal that brought right-handed slugger Donn Clendenon to Shea Stadium. Although the Mets were basically a pitching ballclub built around such arms as Seaver, Jerry Koosman, and Nolan Ryan, they needed some punch. Clendenon helped supply enough to win the pennant and help the Mets take the World Series from the Baltimore Orioles in five games.

When the Mets came back to the Series in 1973, it was due in large measure to another fine deal, the one that brought Rusty Staub from the Montreal Expos in 1972. Staub not only played a key role in the 1973 pennant win but also became the first Met ever to drive in 100 runs in a single season (105 in 1975).

Over the years, there were numerous other deals. Some of them, such as the swap of Ryan (and Don Rose, Leroy Stanton, and Francisco Estrada) for third baseman Jim Fregosi, didn't work out too well.

But others had a material impact on the club. One of these, although it did not lead to a pennant, was the signing of slugger George Foster, who was acquired in a February 1982 trade with the Cincinnati Reds.

Foster had been one of the major cogs in the Big Red Machine, one of the dominant NL teams of the 1970s, and he had had seasons in which he hit 52 and then 40 home runs for the Reds. His acquisition gave the Mets credibility with their fans.

It came about because the team had declined to a sorry state after the championship teams of 1969 and 1973. The club was sold in 1980, and the new owners, a group headed by publisher Nelson Doubleday, wanted a marquee attraction, a major name, to give an indication to the fans that the new ownership was serious about its attempts to rebuild the team into a contender.

To a degree, Foster was a disappointment, in that he never hit more than 28 homers in a season for the Mets, and he did not directly lead the team to a pennant. However, to a great degree his presence (particularly during his first couple of seasons) was important as an expression to the fans and probably achieved its objective.

Of a more material value, though, were the deals in which the Mets acquired first baseman Keith Hernandez (during the 1983 season) and catcher Gary Carter (after the 1984 season). Having been unable to fill either of those positions with a capable, major league–caliber player, the Mets decided to trade for them or acquire them via the free-agent route.

Both Hernandez and Carter produced for the Mets and helped turn the team into a serious championship contender. Both, of course, also played major roles on the 1986 World Series winner and the 1988 NL East champion.

By 1990 both were in the twilights of their careers and were released. But although the Mets allowed them to go to make way for younger talent, Carter and Hernandez had provided the veteran experience and leadership that the Mets had needed to learn how to win in the 1980s.

Behind all the moves of the 1980s was the front office team that was, in itself, a key acquisition.

Rusty Staub

Frank Cashen, formerly with the fine Baltimore Oriole clubs of the 1970s, was working in the commissioner's office in New York when the Doubleday group bought the Mets.

The new owners naturally sought an exprienced baseball man to head up the front office, and Cashen was recommended by commissioner Bowie Kuhn. He then assembled the rest of the player personnel and scouting staff.

One of the more controversial moves of the Cashen regime was its allowing Seaver to be claimed by the Chicago White Sox in January 1984, a year after he had been reacquired by the Mets. The White Sox were due a player in the compensation pool for having lost pitcher Dennis Lamp as a free agent the year before, and they claimed Seaver when the Mets left him unprotected. Cashen and his staff took heavy criticism from the fans and the press for that move, since Seaver was one of the all-time favorites of the Mets' followers.

However, perhaps in compensation, the Mets were to subsequently acquire two very fine pitchers in good deals. One was young Dave Cone from the Kansas City Royals for players who were surplus in New York, and the other was left-hander Frank Viola, a New York native, from the Minnesota Twins.

Viola had been a Cy Young Award winner for the Twins but had gotten into an intense contract squabble with the Minnesota front office and virtually forced a trade.

He turned out to be a very valuable acquisition for the Mets and took up much of the slack when Doc Gooden went through difficult times. Gooden was, of course, the established leader of the Mets' staff.

An irony of the George Foster transaction was that one of the players traded to Cincinnati was catcher Alex Trevino, who subsequently played for several clubs including the Dodgers and the Astros. But in 1990 he was re-signed as a free agent by the Mets. It reminded some observers of the transaction many years before, in the early days of the Mets, when catcher Harry Chiti was traded for a player to be named later—and that player to be named later turned out to be Harry Chiti, who was, in effect, traded for himself.

GREAT MOMENTS

It is probable that the greatest moments in the history of the New York Mets came in 1969, when the team clinched first the National League East title, then the NL pennant, and finally the World Series.

By winning in 1969, the Mets elevated the franchise to a different level and changed forever the expectations of their followers. No more were they the laughable but lovable losers.

Now the team had achieved the maximum of baseball success—and in the process became the first modern expansion team to win a World Series. For all time to come, the Mets' fans would expect their team to be competitive with the rest of the teams in the majors. Never again would losing be acceptable.

When the team did decline in the late 1970s, its once-wondrous attendance declined with it, and a chorus of criticism arose, eventually bringing about the sale of the club.

But 1969 was, for the Mets, the most improbable of all events. Even while it was happening, it sometimes seemed as though it couldn't be happening. A club-record 11-game winning streak started in late May, and the Mets were in the race.

By August 13, however, New York was 9½ games back and seemed to be fading from contention. Then the Mets ripped off 38 wins in 49 games, moved into first place to stay on September 10, and clinched the division with a 6-0 victory over the St. Louis Cardinals on September 24, touching off a wild display of joyous (but slightly destructive) emotion at Shea Stadium.

Two unusual games made indelible impressions on Met fans. On July 9 Tom Seaver retired the first 25 Cubs before Jimmy Qualls singled in the ninth. Even more significant, perhaps, was the game at Shea Stadium on September 15 when the Cardinals' Steve Carlton struck out 19 Mets. But Ron Swoboda hit a pair of solo homers, and the Mets won, 2-1.

Then came the playoffs against the NL West champion Atlanta Braves. What was expected to be a pitching-dominated playoff series turned out to be the exact opposite. Although Seaver, Ron Taylor, and Ryan were winners in the three-game sweep of the Braves, the scores of 9-5, 11-6, and 7-4 were somewhat unexpected.

The World Series was a bit more to form. The Baltimore Orioles beat Seaver in the opening game, 4-1, with a three-run fourth inning. But Jerry Koosman (with ninth-inning relief from Taylor) came back with a two-hitter for a 2-1 win in Game 2, evening the Series.

Back at Shea Stadium, Gary Gentry and Ryan combined on a four-hitter for a 5-0 win in Game 3, and Seaver then won Game 4, 2-1, with a six-hitter. The climax came on October 16, when the Mets overcame a 3-0 deficit for a 5-3 victory behind Koosman to end the Series in five games.

Davey Johnson's fly out ended the Series. Some 15 seasons later, Johnson became the Mets' manager. He managed the club for more than 1,000 games and was the most successful field boss in Met history.

In 1973 the Mets again won the NL East and faced one of baseball's powerhouses, the Cincinnati Reds in the championship series. The Mets took a two-games-to-one lead, but the Reds forced a fifth game with a 2-1, 12-inning victory in Game 4 at Shea Stadium.

The fifth game was almost an anticlimax, as the Mets scored twice in the first inning and four times in the fifth, rolling to a 7-2 win behind Seaver.

Now managed by Yogi Berra, the Mets went to the World Series against the Oakland A's, giving Berra the unique distinction of having managed both the Yankees and the Mets in the World Series.

New York built a three-games-to-two edge in the Series, with Seaver and Jon Matlack primed for the final two games in Oakland. But the A's beat Seaver, 3-1, and shelled Matlack with a four-run third that boosted them to a 5-2 victory in the seventh game.

On May 11, 1972, the Mets acquired Willie Mays for pitcher Charlie Williams and cash. The final season of Mays's 22-year career was 1973, and the Mets allowed him to close out his glorious playing days in the World Series. Mays hit .286 in the Series and contributed an RBI single. (Oddly, though Mays played almost 15 seasons in San Francisco, three of his four Series appearances were in New York uniforms, two with the Giants and one with the Mets.)

It was to be 13 years before the Mets returned to the World Series. That return came in 1986, and the man at the helm was Davey Johnson. But before the Mets could reach the Series, they had to battle their way through an NL championship set with the Houston Astros that bordered on the bizarre.

After splitting the first two games in the Astrodome, the Mets went ahead in the series with a 6-5 victory at Shea on Len Dykstra's two-run, ninth-inning home run. But Houston tied it on Mike Scott's second victory, 3-1, in Game 4.

Nolan Ryan, now with the Astros, and Dwight Gooden dueled to a 1-1 draw through 10 innings in the fifth game, but the Mets finally prevailed in 12, 2-1.

Back at the Astrodome, on October 15, came the wildest game of all, a 16-inning affair won by the Mets, 7-6. The Mets tied it, 3-3, with a three-run ninth. Then New York went ahead, 4-3, in the 14th, only to have the Astros tie it. Another three-run inning in the 16th gave the Mets a 7-4 lead, but Houston scored twice and had the tying run aboard when Jesse Orosco finally got the last out.

In the Series the Mets were one strike away from elimination in Game 6 before Gary Carter singled and Mookie Wilson slashed a twisting ground ball down the first base line in the 10th inning. Wilson's ball squirted through the legs of first baseman Bill Buckner, allowing the winning run to score in the Mets 6-5 victory that forced a seventh game. After a day's delay because of rain, the Mets won their second World Series title on October 27 with an 8-5 win after trailing early in the game, 3-0.

Over the years there have been numerous other memorable moments for the Mets—perhaps a surprising number, considering that, by baseball standards, the team is a relatively young one. The opening of Shea Stadium in 1964; the night Willie Mays faced a packed house there and said "good-bye to America"; Tom Seaver striking out 200 or more hitters nine straight seasons; Casey Stengel, Gil Hodges, Yogi Berra, and Davey Johnson managing.

In 1978 Craig Swan led the NL with a 2.43 ERA but didn't clinch the crown until the final day of the season. He is one of three Met pitchers to lead the NL in ERA. Tom Seaver (1970, '71, and '73) and Dwight Gooden (1985) are the other two.

Despite the bonanza of fine pitchers that the franchise has enjoyed, no Met pitcher has ever thrown a no-hitter. Several, of course, have come close. From 1962 to 1988 the Mets pitched 17 one-hitters.

Rusty Staub became the first Met ever to drive in 100 or more runs in a season with 105 in 1975 and, in a second tour of duty with the Mets, in 1983, had 24 pinch hits and equaled the major league record of 25 pinch-hit RBIs in a season.

In 1985 Dwight Gooden was 24-4, and at age 20 became the youngest winner ever of the Cy Young Award. He had a 14-game winning streak and a 1.53 ERA, a Met club record, breaking the mark of 1.76 set by Tom Seaver in 1971.

In his first season with the Mets, 1985, Gary Carter hit 32 home runs and drove in 100 runs.

Throughout the 1986 season the Mets achieved special distinctions. The team total of 108 wins marked only the ninth time since 1900 that a team in either major league had won as many as 108 games. The division clinching on September 17 (a 4-2 win over the Cubs) was the earliest any NL East team had ever clinched.

In 1987 both Howard Johnson and Darryl Strawberry were 30-30 men, hitting 30 or more homers and stealing 30 or more bases. Strawberry set a club record of 39 home runs. Johnson repeated the 30-30 feat in 1989, becoming only the third man in major league history to achieve the distinction more than once.

Moonwalk, the Sequel: The Mets come from behind to beat
the Red Sox in Game Seven of the World Series and win their
second world championship (October 27, 1986)

ALL TIME ALL STAR TEAM

FIRST BASE ★ ED KRANEPOOL

Although Keith Hernandez was easily the more stylish player at first base, Ed Kranepool was a foundation player for the Mets virtually from their infancy. Kranepool remains the Mets' all-time leader in games played (1,853), in hits (1,418), and in doubles (225), and he is the only Met with 2,000 or more career total bases. In the later years of his career, he became one of the finest pinch-hitters in the majors. He also played leading roles in the Mets' championship team of 1969 and the pennant winner of 1973.

SECOND BASE ★ FELIX MILLAN

For five seasons, Felix Millan was the Mets' regular second baseman and one of the best in the league. During the 1973 pennant drive, Millan also made heavy offensive contributions, batting .290 that season as well as playing a superb second base. Indeed, it was probably the acquisition of Millan in an off-season deal with Atlanta that helped move the Mets from third to first in the standings.

SHORTSTOP ★ BUD HARRELSON

Although he never hit more than .258 for the Mets, Bud Harrelson was the most successful shortstop in Mets' history. His defensive work was critical to both the 1969 and 1973 pennant victories. Indeed, in 1973 his brawl at second base with Pete Rose was credited with helping to inspire the Mets' upset of Cincinnati. Harrelson hit .252 and stole 28 bases in 1971 in perhaps his best all-around year. He became the Mets' manager in May 1990.

THIRD BASE ★ HOWARD JOHNSON

In a position occupied by more than 80 different players in the relatively short history of the franchise, Howard Johnson has become *the* third baseman. Since being acquired by the Mets from the Detroit Tigers in 1984, Johnson has had two 36-homer seasons and in 1989 drove in 101 runs. That season, he also set a Met club record for doubles with 41. Johnson is also one of only three players in major league history (Willie Mays and Bobby Bonds are the others) to have two or more seasons of 30 or more home runs *and* 30 or more stolen bases.

LEFT FIELD ★ CLEON JONES

For nearly a dozen years, Cleon Jones's right-handed bat was a key element in the Mets' pennant chances. Four times in that span, he led the club in batting average, including a career-high .340 in 1969, when the Mets won their first pennant. Jones hit .319 in 1971, and his two best marks represent the two best in Met history. Jones also led the Mets in RBIs twice, triples once, and stolen bases twice. Few, if any, of his contemporaries were his equal when he got on a hot streak at the plate.

CENTER FIELD ★ TOMMIE AGEE

A sometimes brilliant defensive player and a hitter with above-average power, Tommie Agee was a major contributor to the Mets' 1969 world championship—both in winning the pennant and during the World Series. He led the Mets in home runs (26) and RBIs (76) during the 1969 season and also, perhaps more importantly, provided solid and sometimes spectacular defense in center field. His acrobatic catches in the World Series remain a part of almost every Series highlight package.

RIGHT FIELD ★ DARRYL STRAWBERRY

Although there are those who do not believe that Darryl Strawberry has yet reached his potential, he is clearly the best right fielder in the history of the Mets, in addition to being the dominant power hitter in their record book. It took him only seven years to become the first Met to surpass 200 career homers for the club, and he also set single-season marks for home runs. He holds the Mets' club record for career RBIs and extra-base hits. His league-leading 39 home runs were a major factor in the Mets' winning their division in 1988, and his 27 helped win the pennant in 1986.

CATCHER ★ GARY CARTER

In his five seasons with the Mets, Carter helped transform the team from a good one to a serious contender. His handling of pitchers and pure receiving work helped make up for some throwing difficulty. He also made major contributions with his bat, hitting 76 homers and driving in 288 runs in his first three years with the Mets. He produced two clutch homers in the 1986 World Series that helped the Mets to their second world championship. Carter also played some at first base and in the outfield in an effort to get his bat in the lineup when catching injuries began to take their toll.

LEFT-HANDED STARTER ★ JERRY KOOSMAN

Jerry Koosman's 140 wins are the second best career total in Met history, and the same is true for virtually all his other career stats. Koosman pitched 2,545 innings for the Mets, had 108 complete games in 346 starts and a 3.09 career ERA with 1,799 strikeouts. He threw 26 shutouts. In 1968 he was 19-12 and in 1969 17-9, as the Mets rose from ninth to first over the space of two seasons. He was 21-10 in 1976. He also won two games in the 1969 World Series and another in 1973.

RIGHT-HANDED STARTER ★ TOM SEAVER

Easily the most recognizable name on the Mets in the 1960s and 1970s, and often referred to in the local press as "the Franchise," George Thomas Seaver won 198 career games for the Mets (against 124 losses). Virtually every one of his statistics is a club career record, including most innings pitched, complete games (171), gamesstarted (395), games (401), ERA (2.57), strikeouts (2,541), and shutouts (44). Seaver, of course, also pitched with several other clubs (the Reds, the White Sox, and the Red Sox) en route to winning his career total of 311 games.

RELIEF PITCHER ★ TUG MCGRAW

Tug McGraw had 86 career saves for the Mets, the second best in team history. But he can be rated as the team's best reliever for less-solid reasons. In 1973 McGraw created the inspirational cry "You Gotta Believe" for the team, which came on in the closing weeks to win the division and then the NL pennant. In 1972 McGraw saved a career-high 27 games, and in 1973 he added 25 saves. Overall, he pitched 793 innings for the Mets (most of any reliever), and his 47 wins are topped only by starters.

RECORD HOLDERS

CAREER

BATTING

Games	Ed Kranepool	1,853
At-bats	Ed Kranepool	5,436
Batting average	Keith Hernandez	.297
Runs	Darryl Strawberry	662
Hits	Ed Kranepool	1,418
Doubles	Ed Kranepool	225
Triples	Mookie Wilson	62
Home runs	Darryl Strawberry	252
Grand slams	John Milner	5
Total bases	Ed Kranepool	2,047
Slugging percentage	Darryl Strawberry	.520
RBIs	Darryl Strawberry	733
Extra-base hits	Darryl Strawberry	469
Bases on balls	Darryl Strawberry	580
Strikeouts	Darryl Strawberry	960
Stolen bases	Mookie Wilson	281

PITCHING

Games	Tom Seaver	401
Wins	Tom Seaver	198
Losses	Jerry Koosman	137
Starts	Tom Seaver	395
Complete games	Tom Seaver	171
Shutouts	Tom Seaver	44
Innings	Tom Seaver	3,045
ERA	Tom Seaver	2.57
Strikeouts	Tom Seaver	2,541
Walks	Tom Seaver	847
Saves	Jesse Orosco	107
Relief appearances	Jesse Orosco	368
Winning percentage	Dwight Gooden	.721

Tom Seaver

Ed Kranepool

RECORD HOLDERS

SEASON

BATTING

Games	Felix Millan (1975)	162
At-bats	Felix Millan (1975)	676
Batting average	Cleon Jones (1969)	.340
Runs	Darryl Strawberry (1987)	108
Hits	Felix Millan (1975)	191
Doubles	Howard Johnson (1989)	41
Triples	Mookie Wilson (1984)	10
Home runs	Darryl Strawberry (1987 and 1988)	39
Grand slams	John Milner (1976)	3
Total bases	Howard Johnson (1989)	319
Slugging percentage	Darryl Strawberry (1987)	.583
RBIs	Darryl Strawberry (1990)	108
Extra-base hits	Howard Johnson (1989)	80
Bases on balls	Keith Hernandez (1984), Darryl Strawberry (1987)	97
Most strikeouts	Tommie Agee (1970), Dave Kingman (1982)	156
Fewest strikeouts	Felix Millan (1974)	14
Stolen bases	Mookie Wilson (1982)	58

PITCHING

Games	Roger McDowell (1986)	75
Wins	Tom Seaver (1969)	25
Losses	Roger Craig (1962), Jack Fisher (1965)	24
Starts	Tom Seaver (1970, 1973, 1975), Jack Fisher (1965)	36
Complete games	Tom Seaver (1971)	21
Shutouts	Dwight Gooden (1985)	8
Innings	Tom Seaver (1970)	291
ERA	Dwight Gooden (1985)	1.53
Strikeouts	Tom Seaver (1971)	289
Walks	Nolan Ryan (1971)	116
Saves	Jesse Orosco (1984)	31
Relief appearances	Roger McDowell (1986)	75
Winning percentage	Dwight Gooden (1985)	.857

TRIVIA QUIZ

1. Which Met manager got the last hit off Hall of Fame pitcher Sandy Koufax?

2. Prior to 1990 the Mets had only one player whose last name began with the letter "Y." Who was he?

3. In 1962 how many games did the Mets play before they won one?

4. In 1977 the Mets had a playing manager. He later managed the Braves and the Cardinals. Name him.

5. Two Met pitchers have won a total of four Cy Young Awards. Who are they?

6. This man set a Mets' club record for homers in a season that stood for 13 years. Who was he?

7. Only one Met has ever hit more than 200 career home runs for the team. Name him.

8. This Met infielder was a starter in the 1964 All-Star Game. Who was he and what position did he play?

9. What year did the Mets move into Shea Stadium?

10. In the 1969 World Series, this left-hander won games 2 and 5. Name him.

ANSWERS ON PAGE 63

1991 SCHEDULE

APRIL

SUN	MON	TUE	WED	THU	FRI	SAT
	1	2	3	4	5	6 TOR 2:40
7	8 PHI 3:10	9 PHI 1:40	10 PHI 7:40	11 MON 7:40	12 MON 7:40	13 MON 1:40
14 MON 1:40	15 PIT 7:35	16 PIT 7:35	17 PIT 7:35	18	19 MON 7:35	20 MON 1:35
21 MON 1:35	22	23 PHI 7:35	24 PHI 7:35	25 PHI 7:35	26 PIT 7:40	27 PIT 1:40
28 PIT 1:40	29	30 SD 7:40				

MAY

SUN	MON	TUE	WED	THU	FRI	SAT
			1 SD 7:40	2	3 SF 7:40	4 SF 1:40
5 SF 1:40	6	7 LA 7:40	8 LA 7:40	9	10 SF 10:35	11 SF 4:05
12 SF 4:05	13 SD 10:05	14 SD 10:05	15 SD 4:00	16	17 LA 10:35	18 LA 10:05
19 LA 4:05	20	21 CHI 7:40	22 CHI 7:40	23 CHI 7:40	24 STL 7:40	25 STL 1:40
26 STL 1:40	27 CHI 2:20	28 CHI 8:05	29 CHI 2:20	30	31 STL 8:35	

JUNE

SUN	MON	TUE	WED	THU	FRI	SAT
						1 STL 8:05
2 STL 2:15	3	4 CIN 7:35	5 CIN 7:35	6 CIN 7:35	7 HOU 8:35	8 HOU 8:05
9 HOU 2:35	10 HOU 8:35	11 ATL 7:40	12 ATL 7:40	13 ATL 7:40	14 HOU 7:40	15 HOU 7:10
16 HOU 1:40	17 CIN 7:40	18 CIN 7:40	19 CIN 7:40	20 ATL 7:40	21 ATL 7:40	22 ATL 7:10
23 ATL 2:10	24	25 MON 7:40	26 MON 7:40	27 MON 1:40	28 PHI 7:40	29 PHI 7:10
30 PHI 1:40						

▨ Home games   ☐ Road games

JULY

SUN	MON	TUE	WED	THU	FRI	SAT
	1 MON 1:35	2 MON 7:35	3 MON 7:35	4 MON 7:35	5 PHI 7:35	6 PHI 7:05
7 PHI 1:35	8	9 ALL-STAR GAME	10	11 SD 7:40	12 SD 7:40	13 SD 7:10
14 SD 1:40	15 SF 7:40	16 SF 7:40	17 SF 1:40	18 LA 7:40	19 LA 7:40	20 LA 1:40
21 LA 1:40	22	23 SF 10:35	24 SF 10:05	25 SF 3:35	26 SD 10:05	27 SD 10:05
28 SD 4:05	29 LA 10:35	30 LA 10:35	31 LA 10:35			

AUGUST

SUN	MON	TUE	WED	THU	FRI	SAT
				1	2 CHI 7:40	3 CHI 7:10
4 CHI 3:10	5 CHI 7:40	6 PIT 7:40	7 PIT 7:40	8 PIT 1:40	9 CHI 3:20	10 CHI 2:20
11 CHI 2:20	12 CHI 2:20	13 STL 8:35	14 STL 8:35	15 STL 8:35	16 PIT 7:35	17 PIT 7:05
18 PIT 1:35	19	20 STL 7:40	21 STL 7:40	22 STL 7:40	23 CIN 7:40	24 CIN 7:10
25 CIN 1:40	26 HOU 8:35	27 HOU 8:35	28 ATL 7:40	29 ATL 7:40	30 CIN 7:35	31 CIN 7:05

SEPTEMBER

SUN	MON	TUE	WED	THU	FRI	SAT
1 CIN 2:15	2 HOU 1:40	3 HOU 7:40	4 HOU 7:40	5	6 ATL 7:40	7 ATL 1:40
8 ATL 1:40	9 MON 7:40	10 MON 1:40	11 CHI 2:20	12 CHI 2:20	13 STL 8:35	14 STL 8:05
15 STL 2:15	16 MON 7:35	17 MON 7:35	18 CHI 7:40	19 CHI 7:40	20 STL 7:40	21 STL 1:40
22 STL 1:40	23	24 PIT 7:40	25 PIT 7:40	26 PIT 7:40	27 PHI 7:40	28 PHI 1:40
29 PHI 1:40	30 PHI 7:35					

OCTOBER

SUN	MON	TUE	WED	THU	FRI	SAT
		1 PIT 7:35	2 PIT 7:35	3	4 PHI 7:35	5 PHI 7:05
6 PHI 1:35	7	8	9	10	11	12

COLLECTOR'S CORNER

NOTES
&
AUTOGRAPHS

Ain't no fences high enough.

The TPS® "Power End™" is not an experiment like some other "new" bats around town. It's simply the best performing softball bat on the market. It delivers extra bat speed and maximum hitting power with lightweight, but super-strong CU31 alloy. No wonder it's preferred by the most powerful hitters in the game. Better get one, while the fences last.

Louisville Slugger®

HcB Hillerich & Bradsby Co. Louisville, Kentucky
Say yes to sports, say no to drugs!